GONE FOREVER

THE PASSENGER PIGEON

by Susan Dudley Morrison

CRESTWOOD HOUSE
New York

LIBRARY OF CONGRESS CATALOGING IN PUBLICATION DATA

Morrison, Susan Dudley.
The passenger pigeon / by Susan Dudley Morrison
p. cm. – (Gone forever)
Includes index.
SUMMARY: Discusses the history of the Passenger Pigeon, which at one time made up one-quarter of the
birds in America but is now extinct.
1. Passenger pigeons–Juvenile literature. [1. Passenger pigeons. 2. Extinct birds.] I. Title. II. Series.

QL696.C63M67	1989	598'.65–dc20	89-31839
ISBN 0-89686-457-X			CIP
			AC

Photo Credits

DRK Photo: (Don & Pat Valenti) 5, 17, 20, 29, 33; (Stephen J. Krasemann) 15, 32
Photo Researchers, Inc.: (Tom McHugh) 8; (National Audubon Society) 19, 25
The Academy of Natural Sciences of Philadelphia: (Steven Holt) 9, 22, 26, 34; (Doug Wechsler) 13
The Bettmann Archive: 11, 41
Culver Pictures, Inc.: 37, 44

Cover illustration by Kristi Schaeppi

Consultant: Professor Robert E. Sloan, Paleontologist
University of Minnesota

Macmillan Publishing Company
866 Third Avenue
New York, NY 10022
Collier Macmillan Canada, Inc.

CRESTWOOD HOUSE

Produced by Carnival Enterprises

Printed in the United States of America

First Edition

10 9 8 7 6 5 4 3 2 1

Contents

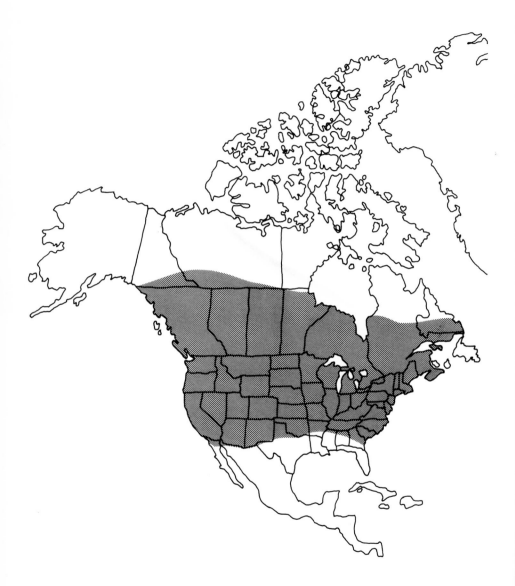

Passenger Pigeons lived throughout North America.

The last Passenger Pigeon died in 1914. Stuffed birds can be seen today in museums.

The Last Day

In the early afternoon of September 1, 1914, Martha, a Passenger Pigeon, died of old age. She might have also died of loneliness, for she was the last Passenger Pigeon in the world.

Martha was part of a flock raised by Professor C. O. Whitman. Years before, a Native American had found two birds. He had given the birds to David Whittaker, a bird lover who lived in Wisconsin. The two birds had a dozen or so offspring, called *squabs*. A few years later, Whittaker

5

sold half the flock to Professor Whitman. From those birds, Martha was born. The bird was named after Martha Washington.

Martha and her brothers and sisters lived in Chicago. The professor took care of the birds and fed them acorns, corn, and worms. He hoped the baby birds would have their own squabs someday. Other people who loved birds hoped the same thing and watched as the squabs grew.

No one could find any other Passenger Pigeons. They looked in the woods where the birds used to live. Some people said they would pay anyone who could find a Passenger Pigeon. One group offered a $1,500 reward. Another offered $5,000 for a pair of the birds in a nest.

A few people thought they saw Passenger Pigeons and tried to claim the rewards. When they described the birds, however, the experts knew they had not seen Passenger Pigeons. The birds the people had seen were Mourning Doves. Mourning Doves look a lot like Passenger Pigeons, but they are smaller.

The years went by. Martha and her brothers and sisters grew older, but they had no squabs. No one had seen a wild Passenger Pigeon since 1899.

One by one, the birds raised by David Whittaker died. With only Martha left, people knew there would soon be no more Passenger Pigeons.

In 1902, Martha was taken to the Cincinnati Zoological Gardens. There, people could see a Passenger Pigeon one last time. For a while, Martha was the most famous bird in the world because there were no other birds like her anywhere. It was too late. They had all died or been killed.

Martha died when she was about 18 years old. Papers around the world wrote of her death. People all over were sad because they knew they had lost something they could never find again.

Some people remembered when Passenger Pigeons used to fill the sky. They couldn't believe the birds were all gone. They thought at first the birds had flown to other lands. But no one has ever seen another Passenger Pigeon again.

After Martha died, her body was frozen. It was shipped to Washington, D.C., where it was stuffed and mounted. People today can see her as she stands in her glass case at the Natural History Museum of the Smithsonian Institution.

Today Passenger Pigeons are *extinct*. That means all of them have died, and no others will ever be born. What happened to them? It's a sad story. But it's a story we can learn from. We can learn how to protect other living things that share our Earth.

A Real Beauty!

Today, we can see Passenger Pigeons only in pictures. A few, like Martha, have been stuffed and put on display in glass cases. Passenger Pigeons were larger than the pigeons we see in parks. A male Passenger Pigeon was 15 to 18 inches long. Its wings spread out 23 to 25 inches. Females were about an inch shorter.

The Passenger Pigeon had shiny blue and violet feathers on its back. The feathers reflected many colors. Farther

The Passenger Pigeon could see for miles with its bright orange eyes.

down on the back, the feathers were brownish gray.

The bird's tail feathers were white except for two dark gray ones in the middle. Each bird had 12 long, pointed tail feathers. Its wings were long and pointed, too. A blue-gray color, they were almost as long as the tail.

The Passenger Pigeon had a small head and neck. The head was blue-gray. Around the eyes and the chin, black blotches could be seen. The breast was red. Female birds, always less colorful, were more gray and brown.

Passenger Pigeons had black beaks that were thin and short. They had red feet. Their bright orange eyes could see for many miles.

Passenger Pigeons were more colorful than the pigeons seen today. This exhibit is at the Field Museum in Chicago.

They had short legs and heavy shoulders. With such a body, it was easier for them to fly than to walk. When they walked, they nodded their heads in a circle.

Flyers of Fame

Passenger Pigeons were known for their flying skills. With their strong wings, they could fly many miles quickly. When they wanted to fly faster, the birds flapped their wings again and again and then glided for a while.

The great bird expert *John James Audubon* figured one flock flew 60 miles an hour. Other bird experts said some birds flew 100 miles an hour.

Because they flew so far, the birds were named Passenger Pigeons. Scientists call them *Ectopistes migratorius*. Both words mean to wander or to change places often. They were also called wild pigeons or wood pigeons. The Narragansett Indians called the birds *wuskowhan,* which means wanderer.

Passenger Pigeons traveled, or *migrated,* in huge flocks. There didn't seem to be any leader. The birds flew in rows, some higher, some lower. Smaller flocks looked like black clouds in the sky. The flocks of young birds flew close to the ground. If the day was windy, the older birds flew lower, too.

As they flew, the birds sometimes met hawks. Hawks fed on pigeons and other birds. To get away from a hawk, dozens of birds would fly toward the center of the flock. They looked like huge, black waves, rippling across the sky.

Many experts believe Passenger Pigeons could fly 60 or even 100 miles an hour.

The birds started their trip in the early morning. After a few hours, they stopped to eat. Then they flew on. By night, they usually had come to the end of their journey.

Pigeons were tough and could stand the cold, but a sudden storm could kill them. Sometimes they froze in the snow. Other times the snow hid their food, and they starved. Young birds often got lost in storms and fog.

When the flock was ready to land, the birds flew down and then back up again. They first landed in nearby trees and then flew to the ground to eat.

All in the Family

The Passenger Pigeon is related to today's doves and pigeons. One of the more famous members of the pigeon family is the *homing pigeon*. Homing pigeons can fly many miles at fast speeds, too. They can also be trained to return home. Even if they are let loose many hundreds of miles away, they will find their homes.

In World War I, homing pigeons were used to carry notes to soldiers in the field, because there was no other way to reach the soldiers. One pigeon saved many troops by bringing help during a battle.

Pigeons were also used in World War II. When pilots took off in planes, pigeons went with them. If the plane crashed, the birds flew for help.

Today, homing pigeons are no longer needed by the army. Soldiers use radio signals to ask for help and to keep in touch with the rest of the world.

There are about 600 types, or *species*, of wild pigeons and doves today. They live all over the world. About 150 of them are tame. They are raised for food or as pets.

Members of a species are very much alike. They mate with each other and almost never mate with members of other species. Even if they do mate with other species, their young can't have offspring.

People have tamed pigeons for thousands of years. Three thousand years before the birth of Christ, the Egyptians taught them to carry messages.

Each species of pigeon has its own special look and way

Six hundred species of wild pigeons and doves are alive today.

of doing things. But never again will there be another species of birds just like the Passenger Pigeon.

What They Ate

Passenger Pigeons did not fly north or south at certain seasons as some birds do. They waited until there wasn't enough food where they were. Then they flew to new spots. The flock flew high overhead, looking for the best feeding grounds. Once they saw a good place, they flew in circles. Then the whole flock swooped down to eat.

Passenger Pigeons ate acorns, nuts, fruits, berries, rice,

13

and grains. They liked beechnuts best of all. The birds found food in farmers' fields, along rivers, and in the woods. They also ate insects and worms. Some ate snails (and their shells). Salt was always favored.

The birds needed to eat lots of food to keep strong. It took great strength to fly quickly over many miles. One bird expert found a bird that had eaten 30 acorns at one time. A second bird had eaten 104 kernels of corn.

When gathering food, the birds in the front of the flock swept along the ground. They tried to collect as much food as they could. Then the birds in the back flew over the ones in front. It was their turn to eat. This went on, with one group flying over the other, until all had finished eating.

In the trees, birds pulled acorns and nuts off with their beaks. They gulped the food down whole. To keep from falling, they flapped their wings backward while pulling on the nuts.

The birds stored the food in their *crops*, sacks in their throats. Then they digested the food slowly. After a big meal, a bird's crop might be as large as an orange.

The birds liked some foods better than others. If they found beechnuts or wheat or corn after a meal, they spit out whatever they had in their crops. Then they ate the tastier nuts or grains.

Like other birds, the pigeons ate sand or fine dirt. It helped digest their food.

When the pigeons drank, they put their heads underwater up to their eyes. They kept their heads under the water until they had drunk all they wanted.

The diet of the Passenger Pigeon included acorns and nuts.

Standing on rocks or the shore, the birds drank from rivers or ponds. They also landed on the water and kept their wings half spread while they drank. They took their baths there, too.

A big flock of Passenger Pigeons could destroy a farmer's crops. The birds ate the farmer's grains and fruits. A large flock could have thousands of birds. They could eat millions of bushels at a time.

Farmers tried many ways to keep the pigeons away. They put up scarecrows. They hung cowbells and tin pans to make noises that scared the birds. One farmer hired a man to stand in the fields and crack a whip at planting time. That kept the birds away until soil could be put over the seeds.

Some farmers shot at the birds. Others used nets to capture them. A few soaked grain in alcohol. When the pigeons ate the grain, they became drunk. Then the farmers could catch the birds and kill them.

A few farmers dug long pits and filled them with wheat. Then they killed the birds as they flew down to eat.

In 1860 farmers began to use a machine that planted seeds under the ground. That stopped the pigeons from eating the seeds.

Roosting

After eating, the Passenger Pigeons sat near each other on branches. Sometimes they flew hundreds of miles to find resting places. They liked woods with big trees the best. In Ohio, the birds rested in swamps.

After flying many miles, Passenger Pigeons would roost together on tree branches.

When they found a good spot, they landed on the trees to rest and sleep. This was called *roosting*.

If food was scarce, the birds flew in small groups. When there was plenty of food, they flew in large ones. Young birds usually flew in big flocks in the summer.

Once they found a roosting spot, a flock claimed it for its own. The birds filled every branch for miles. There were so many birds people couldn't even see the trees. Branches came crashing down because of the weight of so many birds. Other branches were bent to the ground.

Often the birds began to roost just as the sun was setting.

It could take them until midnight to settle. After much noise and flapping of wings, the birds tucked their bills into their breast feathers and went to sleep for the night.

For years afterward, people could tell where a large flock of pigeons had roosted. Small trees and branches were knocked down. Plants were crushed. The whole area looked as if it had been hit by a tornado.

Two feet of dung covered the ground. It killed the roots of the plants and trees and turned the leaves brown. But as long as they could find food, the pigeons came back to the same roosting spot.

Early settlers were glad the pigeons had been there because the birds had helped clear the land and made it easier for the settlers to build their houses. The dung also made the soil fertile. So the settlers' crops grew well.

Mating and Nesting

Passenger Pigeons mated from late March to early fall. Most Passenger Pigeons settled in the north and looked for a place with lots of food. The spot had to be easy to get to and be near water.

Before building their nests, the pigeons mated. To attract the female bird, the male bird flapped his wings at her. He moved his body close to hers. Then he gave her a ''hug'' by hooking his head over her neck. High above the ground, perched in a tall tree, the male courted the female.

For about three days, the male cooed softly to his mate.

This painting by John Audubon shows a male Passenger Pigeon courting the female.

19

The birds sat in pairs in the trees, fluttering their wings. During this time, the male fought off other males. In a loud voice, he warned others to stay away. With his wings, he struck the other birds. This made a loud noise, but it didn't hurt the birds.

The male and female birds worked together to build their nests. The male carried twigs from the woods in his bill. The female used the twigs to build the nest.

Shaped like a saucer, the nest was six to seven inches across. The edges were about two and one half inches high. Some birds took only one day to build their nests. Others took a bit longer.

The nests sat in forks in the trees. From below, the eggs could be seen through the holes in the nests.

The birds liked to have lots of others around while they sat on their eggs. Some trees had as many as fifty to one hundred nests along their branches. Many nesting areas filled thirty or so square miles. They were about ten miles long and three miles wide. The largest nesting spot ever reported was one hundred miles long and three to ten miles wide.

In most cases, female Passenger Pigeons laid one shiny white egg at a time. Taking turns, the male and female birds each sat on the egg to keep it warm. In the early morning, the males flew off in a flock to eat. The feeding ground was not too far away, no more than fifty miles.

By 10 A.M., the males came back to the nest. It was time for the females to eat. While they flew off to look for food, the males sat on the eggs.

During the mating season, male and female Passenger Pigeons sat together in the trees. The male in each pair fought off any other males.

The females were back at the nest by 3 P.M. Soon the males flew off again for a second meal. They came back before sunset. The females had only one meal a day while nesting.

The Young

After two weeks, the eggs hatched. The squabs were usually born between April and the end of September. To keep warm, the squabs stayed under their parents' feathers.

After eight days, the squabs could sit in the nests by themselves. They still needed to be kept warm at night, though.

A Passenger Pigeon squab probably looked like this Rock Dove squab.

The squabs ate by putting their bills into their parents' open mouths. The adult birds gave the squabs the food they had already eaten. It was mixed with a milky liquid from the parent birds. The liquid was called *pigeon milk*. It was found in both males and females.

The pigeons had to keep an eye out for *predators*. Those are birds and animals that eat pigeons. Hawks, buzzards, and eagles often swooped down and snatched squabs from the nests.

The parents took care of their squabs for about two weeks. Once the squabs were big enough to be on their own, the adult birds flew away.

At first, the squabs didn't know what to do. They didn't want to leave the nest. They squealed and squawked for a day or two. At last, the young birds jumped from the nest. They fluttered to the ground.

Life in the nest had been good. The young birds had eaten so well they were fatter than their parents. On the ground, they had trouble flying. Soon, though, they began to lose their baby fat. In three or four days, they could fly well.

At first, the squabs stayed under branches. They wanted to keep away from the hawks. The young birds stayed with other squabs. Soon they all flew off together to find food.

When first born, baby birds had fuzzy down of pale yellow. Later, they looked more like the adult birds, but with paler colors. In late summer or early fall, the young birds lost their baby feathers and grew new ones. This is called *molting*. Adult birds molted in August or September.

By the time the young birds were six months old, they could have their own offspring.

Where They Lived

Before they died out, Passenger Pigeons lived in the forests of North America. They lived between Canada and northern Mississippi and as far west as the Mississippi River. A few were found as far south as Cuba and as far north as northwest Canada.

During the winter, they flew to Arkansas and North Carolina and other states in the South. Summers were spent farther north, in the Northeast and Canada. Many stayed in the Hudson Bay area until December. Then they flew south where there was more food. Large flocks were seen in Ohio, Kentucky, and Indiana.

As more people moved to the Northeast, the birds flew west. Passenger Pigeons formed "pigeon cities" in Michigan and Wisconsin.

The birds liked big forests, rivers, and fields where food grew. They liked hardwood trees the best. Beech, maple, and oak were their favorites. The birds also roosted in spruce, hemlock, and pine trees.

In 1830, John Audubon took 350 Passenger Pigeons to England. He gave them to English bird lovers with lots of land. People hoped the birds would mate there. But they didn't, and later all the birds in England died.

24 *This engraving was based on a portrait of John James Audubon painted in 1833.*

How They Talked

Passenger Pigeons made strange sounds. They cooed like today's pigeons and doves. They also scolded, clucked, and made a noise that sounded like "keck." They often made loud, sharp sounds, too.

The birds told each other when they found food. Other times they scolded an enemy or greeted a friend. They used sounds to warn of hawks and to call their mates. Each sound had a special meaning.

They were so noisy when they built their nests, they could be heard five miles away. The sound they made was a loud twitter.

A loud tweet was their way of saying hello. When an enemy was nearby, they warned others with a low "twee." They also clapped their wings. Then all the other birds did the same. If they wanted to scare away an enemy, they gave a loud, shrill cry.

When caught in a net, the birds cried with fear. They made low chirps when fighting to get free. Then they lay still, as if they were dead.

The softest sound was the coo the male made to his mate. It was a love sound that only she and those close by could hear.

Like today's Mourning Dove, Passenger Pigeons cooed, clucked, and made loud, sharp sounds to communicate with other pigeons.

Birds by the Millions

Long before the settlers came, millions of Passenger Pigeons lived in North America. The land was thick with forests. There the birds lived, feasting on nuts and berries.

Their enemies were hawks and other birds and animals that ate birds as food. The Native Americans who shared the land killed the pigeons, too. They held torches to the trees. Overcome by smoke, the pigeons fell from their nests.

The Native Americans sometimes used nets to trap the birds. Other times, they poked the birds from the trees with long poles. They also shot the birds from the trees with bows and arrows.

After a hunt, the whole tribe fed on pigeons. They cooked the meat in hot ashes or on sticks held over the fire. They dried or smoked the meat they didn't eat, and they used the fat from the squabs as butter.

Native Americans didn't kill the Passenger Pigeons while the birds were hatching their young. They waited until the squabs could fly before they hunted them. That way, some of the baby birds grew up and had more offspring.

Later, explorers told of big flocks of Passenger Pigeons. The French explorer, Jacques Cartier, saw flocks in Canada in the 1530s. Others told of seeing the birds to the south, in Maine and along the Great Lakes.

One bird expert says there may have been three million to five million Passenger Pigeons in America then. In other words, more than one-quarter of the birds in America may

Hawks were one of the Passenger Pigeon's natural enemies.

have been Passenger Pigeons. That means there were more Passenger Pigeons than any other kind of bird.

The first settlers to come from Europe in the early 1600s

also saw plenty of Passenger Pigeons. In 1688, they spoke of seeing flocks with many thousands of birds.

The pigeons were a mixed blessing to the settlers. In hard times, the settlers ate pigeons to keep from starving. Sometimes, they fed pigeons to their pigs and dogs. The pigeons, in turn, ate the settlers' crops.

When they saw huge flocks overhead, some people were afraid. They thought a large flock was a sign of evil. They feared it meant a war would start or a disease would strike.

In the early 1800s, there were still millions of Passenger Pigeons. One man counted 160 flocks passing by in twenty-one minutes. A second man told of a giant flock he had seen. He guessed there were one billion birds in the flock.

So many Passenger Pigeons flew together that they blocked the sun when they passed. Audubon told of one flock that took three days to pass overhead.

Like thunder from a cloud far away, the noise from the birds' flapping wings filled the air. Bird dung fell from the sky like snowflakes, Audubon said.

They may have flown in large flocks to protect themselves from hawks and other enemies. Or the large flocks may have been able to find food better.

There were so many Passenger Pigeons that no one worried about them. Even Audubon, who knew a great deal about birds, saw no danger.

But there was trouble ahead for the Passenger Pigeon. Soon the huge flocks would be just a memory.

Hunters—the Enemy

As more and more people moved to America, cities began to grow. Trees were cut down to build houses. The forests were cleared away to make roads.

Back in 1754, there had been twenty-four acres of land for each person in Massachusetts. By 1850, there were only four acres. That left the Passenger Pigeon with no place to roost or breed and much less food than before. The last large flock left that state in 1851.

Between 1830 and 1860, the Passenger Pigeon left the East. It had become too crowded with people. The birds flew west where there were more trees.

But the birds had a far greater problem than the loss of the forests. Their greatest enemy was not the person with an ax. It was the person with a gun.

Since the days of the Native American hunters, people had killed the birds for food. But the Native Americans had killed only a small part of a flock. With their guns, the new hunters killed thousands of birds.

The hunters planned well for the migrating birds. With guns ready, they lined the riverbanks. As a huge flock dipped lower to feed along the river, the hunters fired. Thousands of birds fell dead. Often the hunters found the spots where the pigeons roosted. They pitched tents at the edge of the woods. Then they waited for the birds to come.

All watched the sky. Far away, they heard the wings of millions of birds. Soon the whole area was in an uproar. Guns fired. Birds cried harsh warnings to their flocks. They made loud clapping sounds with their wings to signal danger. The dead and wounded birds crashed through branches to the ground. The noise was so loud the people in the town three miles away could hear it.

Hunters also killed birds while they nested. Sometimes the birds had just built their nests. They didn't even have a chance to lay their eggs before they were killed.

Squabs too young to fly were shaken from the trees. People with axes chopped down trees to get more squabs. They cut the trees so they would fall on others. Then the hunters could get the squabs from many trees at once.

The hunters had a stockpile of weapons. Some used guns to shoot the birds from their roosts. There were so many

Because Passenger Pigeons nested closely together, hunters could kill many of them with a single shot.

In the mid 1800s, Passenger Pigeons were used for food, soap, medicine, and feather pillows and comforters.

birds huddled together that it was easy to shoot them. Even a poor shot could kill a dozen birds at a time. Young boys liked to try their skill at pigeon hunts.

Other hunters knocked the birds down with tall poles. Like the Native Americans, they used torches to smoke out the pigeons. The dead birds fell in piles on the ground. At sunrise, the hunters took as many birds as they could carry.

Cleaned and cooked, the pigeons made many meals for the town. Extra meat was salted and put in barrels. Pigeon meat was also soaked in spiced apple cider to keep it from spoiling. Breast meat was smoked.

The neck feathers of a Passenger Pigeon were brilliant shades of pink and violet.

Some people used the squab fat for butter. Others made soap from it. A few used pigeon blood and dung as medical cures.

Pigeon feathers kept people warm at night. Women filled quilts and pillows with them. In almost every house, people made some use of pigeons.

The Last of the Passenger Pigeons

In the 1850s, the railroads opened the Midwest. They linked Boston and New York City with the cities along the

Great Lakes. The trains also went to cities along the Mississippi River.

After the Civil War, people built railroads even farther west. In the late 1860s, two teams began work on one railroad. One team started building on the West Coast. It headed east. The other team began its work along the Mississippi River. It headed west.

The two teams met in Utah on May 10, 1869. All the workers and the people at the train company cheered. They had completed the first railroad to cross the country.

The trains sped along the shiny tracks, bringing people to the West. The trains also helped speed the death of the Passenger Pigeon. By 1860, most of the large flocks had flown west. People back East still wanted to eat pigeons. The trains brought the dead birds to New York City where people paid for them and took them home for supper.

Birds had been killed and sold at market for many years. As early as 1805, large ships carried Passenger Pigeons down the Hudson River to markets in New York City. Twenty-five years later, Audubon told of piles of pigeons in the New York City shops.

But in those days, pigeons could be shipped only a short way. They spoiled if the market was too far away. Now on trains, the birds got to market much faster. That meant that many more birds could be killed and sold.

A good pigeon hunter could earn as much as $40 a day. For a dozen birds, he was paid 50 or 60 cents. The price went down to 35 or 40 cents a dozen in towns near where the birds still lived.

The hunters also hired Native Americans to catch birds for them, paying them one cent a bird.

Live birds were worth $1 to $2 a dozen.

A second invention helped the hunters kill more birds. In 1835 Samuel Morse built a model telegraph unit. With it, he could send news to people many miles away. The news was sent over wires.

By 1861 telegraph wires were laid across the country. Using the new device, hunters wired ahead to see where the pigeons were. Then they rode trains to the spot and killed them before they got away.

Pigeon Traps

Hunters used other tricks to catch Passenger Pigeons, too.

One was to stick poles in the ground near feeding areas. When the birds landed on the poles to rest, the hunters shot them. Using big guns, hunters could shoot 100 birds at a time. A cannon killed even more with one shot.

There were many kinds of nets and traps. One trap was a big box propped up with a stick. Birds went under the box to eat bait put there by a hunter. With a pull of a string, the hunter made the box fall on top of the birds.

With nets, hunters caught hundreds of birds at once. Most of the nets were about 6 feet wide and 20 to 30 feet long. The hunter propped the net open with a pole. Then he tied a rope to the pole. When a flock of birds landed on the net, the hunter pulled the rope. That made the pole fall and the net close over the birds.

Hunters often used nets to catch Passenger Pigeons. A net was spread on the ground and, when the birds landed on it, the hunters would pull a rope and close the net.

If the flock was big, the birds lifted the net. Many birds flew out from under it. To stop them, hunters used stakes or rocks to hold down the net.

Hunters hid in huts close by. The huts were made of tree branches covered with leaves. The hunters kept bait, barrels, and gear in them.

.A second type of net was hung in roosting spots. Tied to trees, it hung down to the ground. Once the birds came, the hunters waved torches and threw sticks. That scared the birds and they flew into the net to get away. Then the hunters pulled the net over them to trap them.

Hunters put bait on nets so the birds would land there. They used wheat, corn and acorns—the birds' favorite foods. For two or three days, the hunters watched as the birds ate the bait. Then, when the birds feared no harm, they trapped them.

Sometimes the hunters kept live birds to use as *decoys*. A decoy is an object used to lure others into a trap. First, the hunter blinded a bird by sewing its eyes shut. A skilled hunter with a sharp needle could do this without causing the bird much pain.

Then he tied a rope to the bird's leg. When the flock passed by, the hunter let the bird go. It flew up to join the other birds. Then, when it reached the end of the cord, it fell down to the net. The flock followed to examine the bird and got caught as well.

Hunters also used dead birds and stuffed birds as decoys. They set them up on the nets to look as if they were feeding.

Other hunters tied birds to poles to lure flocks to nets. They tied blinded pigeons to fat poles that looked like stools.

These became known as *stool pigeons*. The name is given today to people who lure others into traps.

The hunter hid in his hut of branches about 40 yards away. He pulled a string to raise and lower the pole and make the bird's wings flutter.

To the birds overhead, it looked as if the stool pigeon

were landing. Thinking the spot was safe, the flock landed on the net below. There they feasted on the corn and wheat that the hunter had put out for them. The hunter then pulled a cord and trapped the birds in the net.

Passenger Pigeons liked the taste of salt, so some hunters put blocks of salt in their nets. The birds landed on the salt and then were caught in the nets.

A few hunters learned how to call pigeons with small whistles.

Once the pigeons were in the nets, they couldn't get out. With finger and thumb, hunters snapped the birds' necks. Some hunters used pliers to break the birds' necks. A few even bit their necks with their teeth.

The hunters put the birds in bags ready to ship East. After that, they set up the nets again. Then they hid in the huts, waiting for another flock.

The best hunters netted thousands of birds a day. One hunter caught 2,500 birds in one day. A second hunter who used salt licks caught 5,000 in a day. In Michigan, one dealer said he sold 175,000 pigeons a year.

The sale of pigeons was big business. In New York, dealers bought and sold more than 100 barrels of pigeons a day. More and more men became hunters. Selling pigeons seemed like an easy way to make money.

In the 1860s and 1870s, armies of pigeon hunters stalked the birds. About 5,000 men hunted pigeons and brought them to market in the early 1880s.

Other people earned money from the sale of pigeons. Workers were paid for each bird they cleaned.

Railroads got $6 to $12 for each barrel of birds they carried. They charged $300 for each carload of live birds.

Passenger Pigeons brought money to many people.

Shooting Pigeons for Sport

Passenger Pigeons were often kept alive to be fattened and sold to markets later.

Live birds were also sold to sports clubs. Club members had contests to see who was the best shot. They kept the birds in traps. This type of sport was known as *trapshooting*.

On the day of the contest, the men took their shotguns to the field. When they were ready to shoot, they opened the traps. The birds flew out, and the men fired. The winners got prizes and money.

Almost all the birds were killed. The few that got away were usually shot by men and boys who lived nearby.

At one time, almost half a million birds a year were used in the pigeon shoots. Many of the shoots were set up by the dealers who sold pigeons.

Laws Too Late

By the middle of the nineteenth century, some people began to worry about the Passenger Pigeon. They knew

By the 1850s, people no longer saw large flocks of Passenger Pigeons.

many birds were being killed, and they missed the big flocks they used to see flying by.

In 1857, they asked the Ohio Senate to pass a law to protect Passenger Pigeons, but the senate voted against it. Most people didn't believe the birds were dying out. There were still some huge flocks with millions of birds. Why did they need protection?

The killing continued. With each nesting season, the flocks got smaller. In 1885, the people of Ohio saw a large flock nesting for the last time.

The huge flocks of pigeons were gone. Smaller and smaller groups came to the nesting spots. Sometimes only two or three pairs of pigeons appeared.

The hunters stopped their netting because there were no longer any flocks to net. After 1884, Passenger Pigeons were rare. People spotted only one or two at a time.

Many people still thought the pigeons weren't in danger. They thought they had flown to other parts of the country. Others thought they had gone to South America. Still others said the birds were killed by sickness or by storms.

Bird experts began to campaign for laws to save the pigeons. The first laws they won helped landowners. They made hunters who killed pigeons on private property pay a fine to the landowner.

Then, in 1862, New York State passed a law to help nesting birds. The law said no one could shoot the birds within one mile of the nests. That was cut to one-quarter of a mile in 1867. Other states passed the same kind of law.

Hunters who lived in other states had to pay for a license to hunt in Pennsylvania. In 1876, Ohio banned hunters from killing pigeons near their roosts. A Massachusetts law said hunters could kill pigeons only in the fall. That law was passed in 1870.

The laws didn't stop the hunters. They kept on killing the

birds. Very few were fined.

In New York, hunters weren't allowed to kill pigeons to sell for food. But in 1881, a group of sportsmen were allowed to order 20,000 live pigeons from the hunters. The sportsmen used the pigeons as targets, killing every one of them.

The sports club's name was the New York Association for the Protection of Fish and Game. It was a strange name for a group that killed so many pigeons for sport.

Most people didn't seem to care. The farmers hated the pigeons because they ate their crops. They spoke against the laws. By the time laws were passed, most of the pigeons had died. In Michigan, for instance, hunters were still allowed to kill pigeons as late as 1874, when they killed one-half million pigeons in four weeks.

Twenty-three years later, Michigan finally passed a law prohibiting anyone from hunting until 1905. But it was too late. Passenger Pigeons were almost gone.

The End

When there were fewer and fewer pigeons, hunters tried even harder to kill the ones they found. People still wanted to buy them. Because the birds were harder to find, people paid more for each one.

By 1889, there were only a few thousand birds left. Flocks in Michigan had fewer than 100 birds. Even so, a few experts still thought the birds would survive.

No one knows for sure when the last wild pigeon died.

44

The last one anyone saw died in September 1899. The young male bird was flying with a flock of Mourning Doves. A hunter shot it in Babcock, Wisconsin.

Why Did They All Die?

How could millions of birds vanish? There are a number of reasons for their extinction. First, the female bird laid only one egg at a time. In most cases, she laid only one egg a season. So when hunters began killing millions of birds, more birds died each year than were born.

Second, Passenger Pigeons lived in big flocks. That made them good targets for hunters. They also mated more efficiently in big flocks. When the flocks got smaller, the birds didn't have as many offspring.

Third, when people cut down the forests where the birds lived, the birds lost their food and shelter.

Fourth, Passenger Pigeons were not able to change their habits to save their lives. If they had split into pairs, for instance, they might have lived where there wasn't much food, and hunters wouldn't have shot so many at one time.

The fifth reason is the major cause of extinction. People killed the Passenger Pigeon. There were no limits to the killings. Birds were killed while nesting. Parent birds were killed, and squabs just born were left to die. Pigeons were hunted and sold even when the birds were almost gone.

Laws have been passed to make sure other birds do not disappear as the Passenger Pigeon did.

Saving Other Species

In the past 150 years, 40 birds and mammals have died out in North America. Others are near extinction.

Some died because they had no place to go when people cleared the land. Others, like the Passenger Pigeons, were killed by people, who sold them at market.

People were shocked when the last Passenger Pigeon died. It made them think about what they must do to save other birds and animals.

Two important things happened in 1885. That year, the United States opened a new office. The office later became the U.S. Fish and Wildlife Service. It began to help protect wildlife in America.

That year, too, *George Bird Grinnell* started the National Audubon Society. He was upset that millions of Passenger Pigeons were killed each year. The group's goal was to fight against such killings.

As the fate of the Passenger Pigeon became known, more people joined the fight. They wanted to save other birds and animals.

President Theodore Roosevelt, who loved the outdoors, was among them. He worked hard to get laws passed to protect wildlife. He helped set up a refuge where animals would be safe from hunters.

In 1910, New York banned the sale of wild bird feathers. Hatmakers had used them for hats. Other states soon passed their own laws.

Hunting laws now limit the number of birds and animals

that can be killed. The laws also protect the young. Hunting is allowed only at certain times of the year.

Animal experts are now capturing some of the animals most in danger. They study them and learn how to help them. Sometimes the animals need help to have offspring. People find them mates. They protect the animals and their young.

If enough young are born, the animals may survive. Sometimes the young can be put back in the wild. Other times they live in parks, where they are protected.

The Passenger Pigeon is gone forever. Never again will anyone see the huge flocks that once blocked the sun. The beautiful bird taught us that life is fragile. Earth's wild things must be protected. If they aren't, then they, like the Passenger Pigeon, will vanish.

For More Information

For more information about the Passenger Pigeon, write to:

The Maine Audubon Society
118 US Rt. 1
Falmouth, ME 04105

The National Audubon Society
950 Third Avenue
New York, NY 10022

Glossary/Index

Audubon, John James 10, 19, 24, 30, 35–great bird expert of the 1800s.

Crops 14–sacks in pigeons' throats used to store food.

Decoy 38–used to lure others into a trap.

Ectopistes migratorius 10–scientific name for the Passenger Pigeon.

Extinct 7, 45, 46–when all have died and no others will be born.

Grinnell, George Bird 46–founder of the National Audubon Society.

Homing pigeon 12–a bird used to deliver messages.

Migrate 10, 31–to travel from one spot to another.

Molt 23–to shed one set of feathers and grow new ones.

Pigeon milk 23–a milky liquid fed by parent birds to squabs.

Predators 23–animals or birds that eat other animals or birds.

Roost 16, 17, 18, 24, 31, 37, 42–to perch on a tree to rest.

Species 12, 13–group of living things that are very much alike. Members of one species almost never mate with members of another species.

Squabs 5, 6, 22, 23, 28, 32, 34, 45–baby pigeons.

Stool pigeon 38–pigeon tied to pole used to lure other pigeons.

Trapshooting 40–shooting pigeons for sport.